ICE HOCKEY

A TRUE BOOK®

by

Christin Ditchfield

Children's Press®

A Division of Scholastic Inc.

New York Toronto London Auckland Sydney
Mexico City New Delhi Hong Kong
Danbury, Connecticut

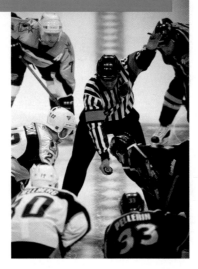

A referee dropping the puck for a face-off

Reading Consultant
Nanci R. Vargus, Ed.D.
Assistant Professor
LIteracy Education
University of Indianapolis
Indianapolis, IN

Library of Congress Cataloging-in-Publication Data

Ditchfield, Christin.
    Ice hockey: a true book / by Christin Ditchfield.
        p. cm.
    Summary: Explores ice hockey, including the history, basic rules,
terminology, and some highlights of the sport.
Includes bibliographical references (p.   ) and index.
    ISBN 0-516-22588-X (lib. bdg.)   0-516-26959-3 (pbk.)
    1. Hockey—Juvenile literature. [1. Hockey.] I. Series. II. Title.
GV847.25 .D58 2003
796.962—dc21

                                                2002009025

CHILDREN'S PRESS, AND A TRUE BOOK®, and associated logos are
trademarks and or registered trademarks of Grolier Publishing Co., Inc.
SCHOLASTIC and associated logos are trademarks and or registered
trademarks of Scholastic Inc.

1 2 3 4 5 6 7 8 9 10 R 12 11 10 09 08 07 06 05 04 03

Contents

No one expected much from the
U.S. ice hockey team during the
1980 Olympic Winter Games.

"Miracle on Ice"

No one thought that the United States ice hockey team would win a medal at the 1980 Olympic Winter Games. Most of the players were college students. In fact, they were the youngest ice-hockey team in Olympic history.

Amazingly, the young U.S. team managed to tie Sweden

and defeat Czechoslovakia, Norway, Romania, and West Germany to reach the semifinals. There they faced their toughest **opponents**—the Soviets.

For nearly thirty years, the Soviet Union had ruled Olympic ice hockey. They captured the gold medal year after year. Their players were older and more experienced than the Americans. The same players who competed on the 1980 Soviet team had won gold medals in 1972 and 1976.

In Lake Placid, New York, the arena was packed with fans. Millions more watched on television. The Soviets quickly scored the first point of the game. It looked like they were headed for an easy win. Five

U.S. goalie Jim Craig protects the goal while playing against the Soviets at the 1980 Olympics.

minutes later, the U.S. team tied the game. The American crowd went wild. Waving banners and flags, they shouted, "U-S-A, U-S-A!"

Out on the ice, the two teams fought hard. As the last period of the game began, the score was tied 3-3. Suddenly, U.S. player Mike Eruzione broke through the Soviet defenders. He fired a shot past the Soviet goaltender and into the net. Minutes later, the United States won the game, 4-3. A television

The Soviet team offers congratulations after the U.S. team's surprising win.

announcer asked viewers around the world, "Do you believe in miracles?"

After their incredible victory in the semifinals, the U.S. team went on to defeat Finland 4-2

in the final round. For the first time in twenty years, an American team had won a gold medal in ice hockey. Their victory would be celebrated as one of the greatest moments in Olympic history, a "Miracle on Ice."

How Hockey Began

From the earliest times, people have used tree branches, clubs, or sticks to hit small objects back and forth for fun. A two-thousand-year-old painting in Greece shows two men with sticks in their hands and a ball on the ground in between them!

Ice hockey as we know it began in Canada in the 1800s.

During the 1800s, many people began playing stick-and-ball games in the winter on frozen lakes and ponds. They wore skates to help them slide quickly across the ice.

Some college students in Canada decided to organize

one of these games. They bor-
rowed rules from such sports as
field hockey, lacrosse, polo, and
soccer. The students called
their new game "ice hockey."

Victoria Rink in Montreal,
Canada, was the center of
the fast-growing hockey
world in the 1890s.

The speed and power of the game made it fun to watch—and play. In no time at all, other colleges had organized hockey teams of their own. Athletes all over Canada and the United States joined hockey leagues.

Lord Stanley, Canada's governor general, loved to watch ice hockey. In 1893, Lord Stanley awarded a special trophy to the best hockey team in Canada. The Stanley Cup soon became

Lord Stanley (left) thought a trophy should be given annually to the best team in hockey. In 1893, the Montreal Amateur Athletic Association became the first Stanley Cup champions (above).

the most famous trophy in North American sports. The National Hockey League (NHL), a **professional** league made up of teams from Canada and the United States, was formed in 1917. Over the next few years, NHL teams competed against teams of several other leagues for the Stanley Cup. By 1926, the other leagues had closed down. Ever since then, the Stanley Cup has been awarded each spring to the champions of the NHL.

Today, more than a million people around the world play

A youth-league hockey
game in Tampa Bay, Florida

ice hockey. Players of all ages
enjoy the thrill of competing
in this exciting, high-energy
game.

The Equipment

In a game of ice hockey, two teams compete on a large "field" of ice called a rink. A rink is usually 200 feet (61 meters) long and 85 to 100 feet (26 to 30.5 m) wide. A red line runs across the center of the rink. In the middle of this line is one of five

An overhead view of an NHL hockey rink

"face-off" circles. This is where play begins. On each side of the red line is a blue line. These two lines divide the rink into three zones.

The center area between the blue lines is called the "neutral zone." Outside the blue lines, each team has a "defending zone" on the side of the rink where their goal sits. The opposite side of the rink, near their opponent's goal, is the "attacking zone."

Players wear steel skates to help them glide up and down the ice. They carry long, narrow sticks made of wood or **fiberglass**. Each hockey

Players use the blades of their hockey sticks to send the puck across the ice.

stick has a flat blade at the bottom. Players use the blades of their hockey sticks to hit a small, round piece of rubber called a puck.

Ice hockey can be a danger-ous sport. Players race across the ice at high speeds. Often, they slam into each other or the wall that surrounds the rink.

Sometimes players trip or fall. A player might get hit by someone else's hockey stick. When the puck is hit, it flies through the air at speeds of over 100 miles (161 kilometers) per hour. If it accidentally hits a player, it can cause serious injuries.

Hockey can be dangerous.
Players sometimes trip or fall.

For safety, all hockey players
wear protective padding. This
includes shin guards, padded
pants, elbow pads, shoulder
pads, and gloves. All players
wear helmets, and many wear

Hockey players, such as this member of the U.S. Olympic women's team, wear lots of safety equipment.

face guards. Mouth guards keep players from biting down on their cheeks or tongues during a fall.

Players who protect the goal area are called goaltenders or goalies. They often use their bodies to block shots from entering the goal. For this reason, goaltenders wear even more padding than other players. They also wear two different gloves: one for blocking shots and one for catching shots.

Goalies wear two different kinds of gloves: one for blocking the puck and one for catching the puck.

The Game

Each team in hockey has six players on the ice. The goal-tender protects the team's goal. He or she tries to keep the opponent's shots from crossing the goal line into the net.

Two teammates skate nearby to help protect the

A goalie and a defenseman try to stop an opponent from scoring.

goal. They are called defensemen. In the middle of the ice, the left wing, right wing, and center lead the attack. These three players, known together as the

A left wing gets ready to pass while being chased by members of the opposing team.

forwards, pass the puck back and forth, shooting it at the other team's goal. Each goal scores one point.

In a professional hockey game, players compete for 60 minutes. The game is divided into three 20-minute periods. When the third period ends, the team with the highest score wins. If both teams have the same number of points, they play 5 minutes of over-time. If no one scores within that time, the game is declared a tie.

The referee and linesmen make sure the players follow

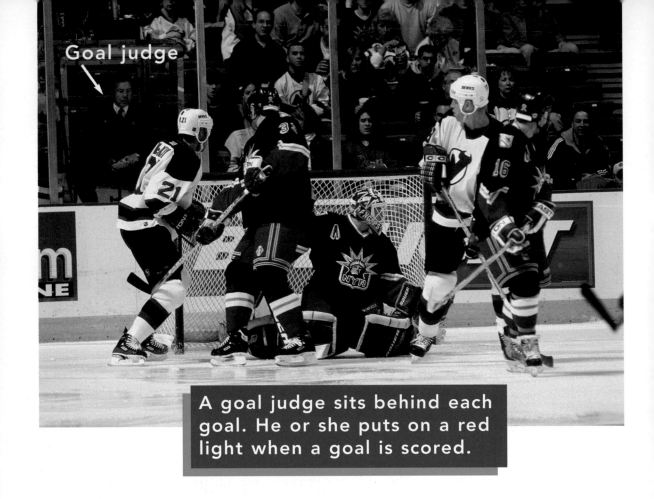

Goal judge

A goal judge sits behind each goal. He or she puts on a red light when a goal is scored.

the rules. Goal judges watch the goal lines carefully to see if goals have been properly scored. An official scorer keeps track of the points scored, and a timekeeper keeps track of the game time. Each game begins with a face-off in the center circle. An official drops the puck between two players from

Every hockey game begins with a face-off.

opposing teams. Each player tries to take control of the puck. Face-offs also take place if the puck is hit out of the rink or stopped by the goalie, or if a violation or penalty is called.

The linesmen call violations when players break certain rules of the game. The two most common violations in hockey are "offsides" and "icing." Offsides is called when an **offensive** player moves into the attacking zone before the puck does or hits

Offsides

Offensive player offsides

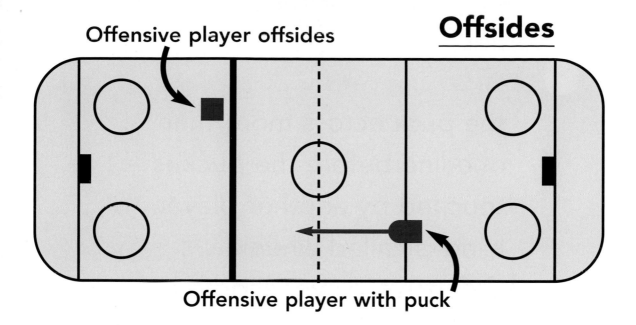

Offensive player with puck

These two diagrams show overhead views of the violations offsides (top) and icing (bottom).

Icing

Defensive player icing puck

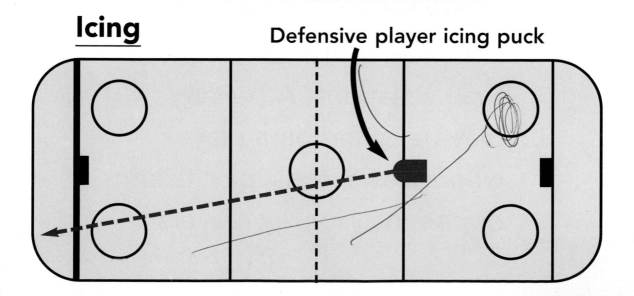

the puck across more than one line before the puck is touched by another player. Icing is called when a **defensive** player shoots the puck from his or her half of the ice across the red center line and beyond the goal line of the opposing team.

Penalties are more serious than violations. A penalty may be called on a player who elbows, trips, or hits an opponent. Hockey players

Hockey penalties include tripping (below) and purposely slamming an opponent into the wall, called boarding (right).

often get into fights because the competition is intense. Although some people think fighting is just a part of the game, it is strictly against the rules.

A player who receives a penalty must leave the ice. For a minor penalty, such as tripping, the player sits in the penalty box for two minutes or until the other team scores. For a major penalty, such as fighting, the player has to sit

out for five minutes. While a
player is in the penalty box,
his or her team is left without
a player in that position.

The Competition

Men and women all over the world play ice hockey. Boys and girls learn to play in youth leagues. High-school and college teams compete against other schools in local, state, and national **tournaments**. Some people play hockey because it's fun and they enjoy

A player in a youth hockey league taking part in a practice drill (left) and a high-school girls' state hockey tournament (below)

the exercise. Others love the thrill of intense competition.

The world's best players compete in the National Hockey League. The NHL has more than thirty teams, located in cities in the United States and Canada. At first, most of the players came from Canada and the United States. Now many more Europeans compete in the NHL.

The most **prestigious** hockey competition is the World Championship Cup, also called the Stanley Cup. Hockey is also an important part of the

In 1998, women's ice hockey became an official Olympic sport. That year, the gold medal went to the U.S. team.

Olympic Winter Games. Men have competed in Olympic ice hockey since 1920. In 1998, women's ice hockey became an official Olympic sport.

The Great One

Wayne Gretzky will probably go down in history as the greatest hockey player of all time. Nicknamed The Great One, Gretzky played 1,487 games in twenty seasons of professional ice hockey. During his incredible career, he set dozens of records and earned all kinds of awards and honors. Gretzky won ten scoring titles

Gretzky in action

and earned nine "Most Valuable Player" awards. He led his teams to four Stanley Cups.

In addition to his awesome talent, Gretzky showed great **sportsmanship**. He refused to get into fights on the ice. He willingly shared the spotlight with his teammates. He treated others with kindness and respect. Gretzky retired from professional hockey in 1999.

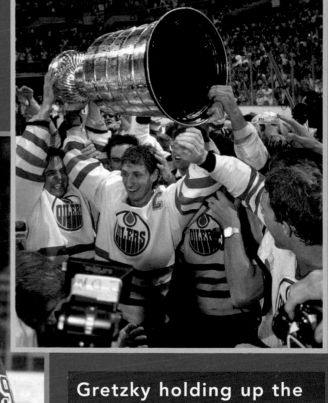

Gretzky holding up the Stanley Cup (above) and Gretzky at the end of his last NHL game (left)

To Find Out More

Here are some additional resources to help you learn more about the game of ice hockey:

 **Books**

Daccord, Brian. **Hockey Goaltending.** Human Kinetics Publishers, 1998.

Diamond, Dan. **Hockey Rules! The Official Illustrated Kids' Guide to NHL Rules and Fundamentals.** Somerville House Books, Ltd., 2001.

Sias, John. **Kids' Book of Hockey: Skills, Strategies, Equipment, and the Rules of the Game.** Carol Publishing Group, 1997.

Weekes, Don. **Rockin' Hockey Trivia: Games, Puzzles, Quizzes.** Douglas & McIntyre, Ltd., 2000.

☀️ Organizations and Online Sites

The Hockey Hall of Fame
30 Yonge Street
Ontario, Canada M5E IX8
http://www.hhof.com

This is the website of an organization dedicated to recording and celebrating the history of the game.

International Ice Hockey Federation
Parkring 11
8002 Zurich
Switzerland
http://www.iihf.com

The IIHF is a group made up of national hockey associations for both men and women.

National Hockey League
1251 Avenue of the Americas
New York, NY 10020
http://www.nhl.com

The official website of the National Hockey League includes all the latest news and information about professional hockey, including team statistics and standings, as well as a special page for kids.

Important Words

defensive describing players trying to keep the other team from scoring

fiberglass strong material made up of tiny glass fibers

offensive describing players trying to score

opponents the players one competes against in a contest or game

prestigious important, highly respected

professional being skilled enough at something to earn money for doing it

sportsmanship good qualities in an athlete such as fairness, respect for one's opponent, and graciousness in both winning and losing

tournaments series of games or contests in which teams compete to win championships

Index

47

Meet the Author

Christin Ditchfield is the author of more than twenty books for children, including nine True Books on sports. A former elementary-school teacher, she is now a freelance writer, conference speaker, and host of the nationally syndicated radio program *Take It To Heart!* Ms. Ditchfield makes her home in Sarasota, Florida.